Queen Victoria's Interesting Bits

and a feast of Victorian facts.

by
Fay Gregory

Barker Books

Barker Books, "White House", The Warren, Ashtead, Surrey, England.

Queen Victoria's Interesting Bits

First Published 1994
Reprinted 1994

Printed in Great Britain by Abbey Green Printers, Chertsey, Surrey.

Contents

Introduction

Everyone's heard of Queen Victoria, the short fat one who was never amused. But did you know that she played billiards, was frightened of bishops and transmitted haemophilia to her children?

Victoria's reign was long and prosperous and this book covers important and noteworthy events which occurred during her sixty-four years on the throne. There are bits about food, clothes, wars and Christmas; did you know that Christmas crackers were a Victorian invention?

Read it just for fun or to help with study. With over one hundred illustrations you'll never say that <u>you</u> were not amused.

Timeline

1819	Victoria born
1837	Death of William IV.
1838	Victoria is crowned.
1840	Victoria marries Albert.
1842	Mines Act prevents women and children working in mines.
1845	Work begins on Osborne House, Isle of Wight.
1847	Factory Act. Workers get Saturday afternoon off.
1851	Great Exhibition.
1854-56	Crimean War.
1857-8	Indian Mutiny.
1861	Death of Albert
1869	Suez Canal opens.
1870	Education Act requires schools to be built Barnardo's home opens. Death of Charles Dickens.
1875	Plimsoll Line
1888	Jack the Ripper murders 5 women.
1891	Education is made free and compulsory.
1896	Olympic Games restarted.
1899 -1902	Boer War.
1901	Death of Victoria.

Queen Victoria's Interesting Bits

Victoria succeeded her uncle, William IV, and took the throne when she was only 18. As a young woman she was pretty, cheerful and outgoing. She was also stubborn, rather sentimental and so prone to tempers and tears that people feared she might end up the same as her loony grandpa, George III. Physically she was very short, less than 5 feet tall, and rather plump. She was typical of well-to-do Victorians, taking lessons in art (which she enjoyed), singing, dancing and the piano (which she didn't).

Victoria married her German cousin, Albert and at first glance they do not seem to have been particularly well matched. She enjoyed going to town and staying up late, whilst he preferred to be out in the country and to go to bed early. She liked light novels and gossip, but he preferred the conversation of intellectuals.

Victoria proposed to Albert because it wouldn't have been proper for him to ask her.

They did share a love of dogs and chess and presumably found other things to like about each other because they had nine children.

Victoria wasn't at all happy about having so many children. She said it made her feel like a cow and that babies reminded her of frogs.

"Ah, he looks just like his Dad".

Throughout her life, Victoria had a man to lean on. When she took the throne, it was her Prime Minister, Lord Melbourne. Albert came next and after he died, John Brown, a servant from Balmoral, took his place. The public didn't know what to think and she had "Mrs. Melbourne" and later "Mrs. Brown" shouted at her. Despite this, Victoria and her family brought respectability back to royalty and made the family an almost sacred institution.

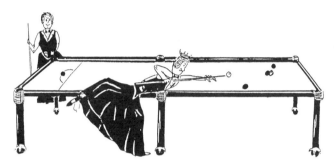

The queen played billiards with her ladies.

Apart from Windsor Castle and Buckingham Palace, Victoria and Albert acquired two other residences, Osborne House on the Isle of Wight, and Balmoral in Scotland, where the royal family became more Scottish than the Scots. Albert learnt Gaelic, everything was tartan, from clothes to carpets to curtains, and they all learned Scottish dancing.

Victoria was well known for her love of fresh air inside the house as well as out. Her servants sometimes lit fires while she was out and had to douse them hurriedly if she came back unexpectedly.

Open the window, Smithers. It's too hot in here.

Smoking was banned in all Victoria's residences and a special room was built onto Osborne House so that her son Bertie could smoke with his friends. It was the only room not to have Victoria's monogram over the door.

A German count was desperate for a smoke and, knowing that this was banned in Windsor Castle, tried to prevent any tell-tale smoke by lying with his head inside the fireplace.

"Can't be too careful, Your Highness.".

Victoria was a carrier of the disease haemophilia which means that when you bleed it doesn't stop. Victoria's son, Leopold, suffered from it and, as a child, was forbidden to do anything that might risk injury. He eventually died of a brain haemorrhage. Three of his sisters transmitted the disease to a large number of European royal families when they married.

Another fascinating fact about Queen Victoria was that from an early age she had a phobia about Bishops.

8

During her lifetime, the queen was attacked seven times, once by a man who hit her over the head with his cane and 6 times by teenage boys carrying guns (although on only one occasion was the gun loaded).

Victoria adored Albert and when she was widowed at 42 it affected her very badly. She wore black for the rest of her life and annoyed her subjects by refusing to perform official duties for 10 years. After his death she is said to have communicated with his spirit through a medium and to have insisted that fresh water and clothes be put in his room each day.

She commissioned numerous paintings and busts of him and, by erecting statues and memorials all over the country, ensured that the people wouldn't forget the Prince. One such memorial was the Albert Memorial in Kensington, London, which includes an angel holding a catalogue from Albert's most famous achievement, the Great Exhibition.

The Albert Memorial.

Queen Victoria died after a period of illness in Osborne House, her country home on the Isle of Wight. She was 81, and had ruled for 63 years, the longest reign ever.

Prince Albert's Interesting Bits

Albert was sensible and kind and Victoria found his fair hair and blue eyes extremely attractive, saying that he had "a delightful exterior". He enjoyed the outdoors (except that he suffered terrible sea-sickness) and was an excellent shot and an accomplished hunter and rider.

Albert was a keen bee keeper.

Other outdoor interests included botany and bee-keeping. Indoors he loved mimicking others, practical jokes, dancing and music. The composer Mendelssohn, a friend of the royal family, was impressed by Albert's efforts at composition.

Albert had a full-size Swiss chalet built in the grounds of Osborne House, where the children were taught to cook, and to grow and sell vegetables for business. He was an enthusiastic father and enjoyed taking his children skating and tobogganing.

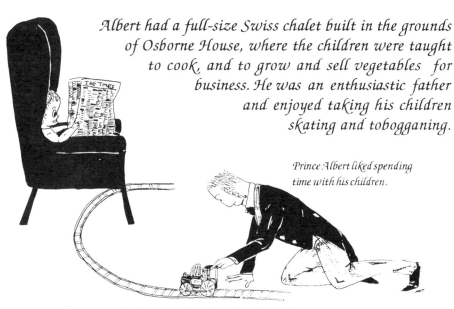

Prince Albert liked spending time with his children.

Albert nearly drowned when he skated on an ornamental pond at Buckingham Palace and the ice gave way.

Albert had a very strong sense of duty and worked very hard for Great Britain, even though he wasn't British himself (he was German). Some say he worked himself into an early grave. He reorganised Buckingham Palace and made it run more economically but his most famous accomplishment was the Great Exhibition of 1851. It was a huge success and he used the resulting £250,000 profits to set up museums in South Kensington, London.

Albert loved hunting, but he wasn't very keen on crawling flat on his stomach through wet Scottish heather. In order to keep his clothes clean and tidy and yet remain

Albert out hunting.

hidden from the view of possible targets, a ditch five feet deep and a mile long was dug in the grounds of Balmoral. After his death, Victoria had a memorial placed where he had shot his last stag.

The young Albert

Prince Albert fell ill with typhoid which was probably caught as a result of the dreadful plumbing at Windsor. At first he refused to stop work but eventually had to give in. After weeks of fever he died on December 14th. 1861 at the age of 42. He was buried in a specially built mausoleum near Windsor, and Victoria joined him there 39 years later.

Interesting Healthy Bits

Although things were improving fast, Victorian health care was still fairly basic. Leeches were in common use in doctors' surgeries to suck blood from the patients (believe it or not, they're still used today), and red hot irons were being used to clean wounds and kill nerves in troublesome teeth.

Smallpox, along with typhoid and cholera (both water-borne diseases), was everywhere, most particularly in the crowded and insanitary city slums. However, lack of sanitation wasn't just for the poor, and an extremely smelly Windsor Castle didn't get its first drains until 1840. Health improved after 1875 when councils became responsible

...actually, I think it's just cured itself!

for drains, sewage, street cleaning and the provision of fresh water. Before toilets became common, men called "undertakers" collected everything nasty and smelly during the night and later sold it as fertiliser.

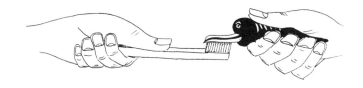

If you want to use a leech again, you just squeeze it like a tube of toothpaste.

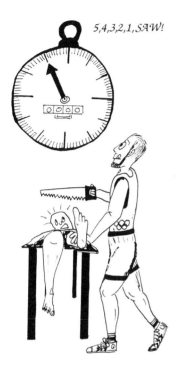

5,4,3,2,1,SAW!

Good surgeons were fast surgeons.

Early in Victoria's reign, there were no anaesthetics and patients had to be held down or heavily dosed with brandy during operations. It's not surprising therefore, that the surgeon's skill was measured in seconds. One surgeon, Robert Liston, expected to take three minutes to amputate a leg, but once managed it in just 28 seconds.

James Simpson (1811-70) tried chloroform on animals before deciding it needed testing on humans. He invited two assistants round for dinner and told his wife to leave them alone for exactly two hours. The three of them sniffed the chloroform and, when she returned two hours later, she found them unconscious.

Not everyone approved of using chloroform, but when Victoria used it at the birth of her eighth child, it became much more widely accepted.

Testing chloroform

Until Louis Pasteur (1825-95) proved the existence of microscopic germs, surgeons were working in everyday clothes without washing hands or instruments. From Pasteur came "Pasteurisation", a process of heating and sterilising still used today in milk production.

Early attempts at pasteurising milk.

Joseph Lister (1827-1912) was a surgeon working in Scotland when he read about Pasteur's work. At that time many patients died a few days after an apparently successful operation and Lister thought that germs might be the cause of this. He began to use antiseptics to treat wounds and, after some initial scepticism, other surgeons accepted his theories. Gradually, more and more patients survived their operations.

Other advances included the arrival of X-rays in Germany (1895), the aspirin (1899), the hypodermic syringe (1853), and a new style of stethoscope which plugged into both ears instead of just one (1850); all a big change from the old days when pills were made with spiders' webs.

Syringes came in very useful for all sorts of things.

Florence Nightingale's Interesting Bits

Florence Nightingale (1820-1910), "the Lady of the Lamp", heard inner voices calling her to do God's work, but it was 7 years before she decided to become a nurse against her family's wishes.

I wish she'd put that lamp out.

Florence went to Scutari, in present day Turkey, where England was fighting the Crimean War. Conditions were atrocious; wounded soldiers lay on filthy floors in rat-infested wards, blocked toilets overflowed into the wards and there was hardly any food. In fact, the soldiers were more likely to die from disease than from their wounds.

Florence insisted that her wards were kept clean, but when she heard about Lister's work on antiseptics she wasn't convinced saying, "Germs! I've never seen them".

Florence Nightingale

Despite hostility from the doctors, Florence and her team of nurses created a successful hospital. She returned to England a reluctant heroine, keeping such a low profile many thought she had died. She spent the rest of her long life improving medical care from an invalid couch. Florence was the first woman to be awarded the Order of Merit.

15

Interesting Transport Bits

Trains arrived before Victoria's reign began, but passengers were not carried until 1825. Most people travelled third class which meant sitting on a wooden bench in a roofless carriage. With the smoke and soot from the engine and bad weather, the ride could be really unpleasant; one passenger died of exposure on his way to the Great Exhibition.

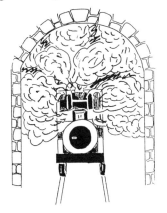

Steam engines were used underground until 1890 when electric trains took over and everyone could breathe again.

Britain was the first country to have a rail network and cheap fares meant people and their goods could travel more easily and quickly. As a result, towns developed as centres of work and the rush-hour arrived. Steam-trams, horse-drawn carriages, carts and buses all competed for road space and, to ease London traffic jams, the first underground line (the Metropolitan) was opened in 1862.

The first fatal railway accident happened in 1830 when William Huskisson, an M.P. who had been inspecting an engine, didn't get out of the way quickly enough. The train ran over his legs and he died of his injuries later.

"What train?"

I told you to go before we left!

Victoria approved of trains because they were so much smoother (she didn't travel third class, mind you) and because crowds couldn't slow her journey by gathering around the carriage.

Things were pretty desperate until the first toilets were installed in trains in the 1870s.

For shorter journeys, the bicycle became a popular mode of transport. The hobby-horse which men pushed along with their feet (women didn't ride the early bicycles) was improved by a Scot, Kirkpatrick Macmillan, who developed a type of forward-and-back crank pedal.

The round-and-round pedals we use now arrived about 1885 and three years later, John Dunlop (another Scot) patented an air-filled tyre which made riding on bumpy roads much more bearable.

Everyone recognises the Penny-Farthing. It appeared in 1870 and was known then as an "Ordinary".

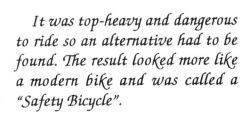

It was top-heavy and dangerous to ride so an alternative had to be found. The result looked more like a modern bike and was called a "Safety Bicycle".

The real reason why Victorians didn't have 50p pieces.

17

Petrol cars appeared in 1885 with the German Karl Benz leading the way. In Britain, there had already been successful experiments with steam cars and coaches but these had been discouraged by the Red Flag Act of 1878. This decreed that a man carrying a red flag had to walk 60 yards ahead of every motor vehicle.

Early cars looked just like horse-drawn carriages without the horse.

The arrival of cars, bikes and trains signalled the end of horse-drawn transport.

Air travel didn't take off until after Victoria's death, (although air balloons were used for observation during the Boer war) and Sir George Cayley made considerable progress working with rotors and the science of flight. He succeeded in producing a glider which carried a boy for a short distance.

Isambard Kingdom Brunel's "Great Western" was one of the first ships to cross the Atlantic under steam but paddle-driven steamers, with their large, uneconomic engines, were slow and expensive so they carried a full set of sails and raised them whenever possible. As steamers needed frequent and time-consuming refuelling stops, sailing ships continued to be used for long journeys until the Suez Canal opened in 1869.

18

Most steamers were built of wood until 1843 when Brunel's large iron ship "Great Britain" was built. Brunel was also the engineer of the "Great Eastern", the largest ship of its time and a ship with a spooky story.

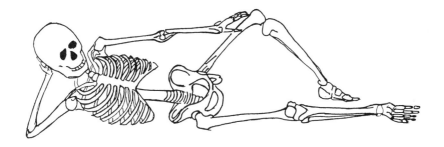

People said the ship was jinxed and when the ship was finally scrapped the bodies of two trapped riveters were rumoured to have been found. All most unlikely!

In 1879, iron gave way to steel which was stronger but also cheaper and lighter (and therefore faster). Another great change was in 1894 when the first turbine reached the engine room. Officially this idea had met with little enthusiasm, until "Turbinia" gate-crashed a naval review and ran circles round the warships. Such speed couldn't be ignored and turbine-driven ships were ordered for the fleet.

The turbine-driven Turbinia showing what she could do.

Engineers' Interesting Bits

George Stephenson (1781-1848) and his son Robert were responsible for the world's first passenger railway service and for miles and miles of railway track. Parliament said that every railway had to use the gauge set by Stephenson (all, that is, except Brunel's railway) and, as Britain was at the forefront of railway construction, Stephenson's gauge was adopted by most of the world.

In 1825, George drove his engine "Locomotion" on its first run. Thirty-three wagons carried goods and passengers and by the end of the journey, an extra 150 passengers had jumped on; not too difficult as the top speed was only 12 m.p.h.. The Stephenson's engine "Rocket" won speed trials in 1829 by travelling at almost 30 m.p.h..

Isambard Kingdom Brunel (1806-1859) was a great engineer and his achievements include the Clifton suspension bridge in Bristol, the Great Western Railway, Paddington railway station and the Thames Tunnel (Rotherhithe to Wapping), as well as the steamships mentioned earlier.

Isambard Kingdom Brunel

Stand clear, I won't be surprised if more than just a coin pops out.

Brunel once got a coin caught in his throat during a trick so he invented some extra-long forceps to remove it. Unfortunately, these didn't work so he designed another apparatus which spun him round and round until the coin popped out.

Interesting Musical Bits

The saxophone was invented in 1846 by a Belgian instrument-maker, Adolphe Saxe. Another new instrument was the sousaphone, inspired by the American "March King", J.P. Sousa.

The upper classes, especially the ladies, were expected to play an instrument, usually the piano, and even if they weren't very good they would play or sing at musical evenings. Those who couldn't perform musically might read aloud or recite poetry to entertain their guests.

Sssshhhh! Not on a Sunday.

There was no entertainment at all on Sundays and although Lord Shaftesbury campaigned for shorter working hours, he wasn't keen on people enjoying themselves on their day off. Eventually, the government allowed bands to play in parks on Sundays, but Shaftesbury fought it all the way.

Victorians loved to visit Music Halls which began around 1850. There, families could see variety shows with jugglers, magicians, dancers, comedians and singers like the famous Marie Lloyd.

Two very well-known British composers were W.S. Gilbert and Arthur Sullivan. Together they wrote light-hearted operas including "The Mikado" and "The Pirates of Penzance". Queen Victoria loved all opera and ballet and even took singing lessons from an opera singer. Prominent composers abroad included Brahms, Chopin, Bizet, and Saint-Saëns who wrote "The Carnival of the Animals".

21

Interesting Bits about Poor Children

If you were born into a poor Victorian family, life was very hard. Most working class fathers weren't paid enough to support their families, so they had to send their children to work. It was common for boys and girls of eight years or even less, to work in coal mines cutting and carrying coal. In 1840 Lord Shaftesbury persuaded the government to investigate the working conditions of children in mines; he even went down pits to see for himself. Two years later the Mines Act made it illegal for children under 10 years old and all women to work underground.

This is the pits!

In 1833, before Victoria came to the throne, a Factory Act (again introduced by Shaftesbury) reduced the number of hours children were allowed to work. For instance, under-thirteens were only allowed to work 48 hours per week. If you were between 13 and 18 you weren't allowed to work more than 69 hours per week; that's over 11 hours a day!

Working such very long hours with dangerous machinery, meant that many children were injured or even killed because they fell asleep on the job.

In big cities, it was not uncommon to find dead babies in the streets because their parents couldn't afford to bury them. One dead baby was even found in a cupboard with the bread!

Hundreds of orphans slept rough and either stole money for food or tried to earn pennies by sweeping horse-dung from the streets. Dr. Barnardo was shocked by what he saw on the London streets and founded his first home for destitute boys in 1870.

With all this manure about, you'd think I'd have grown a bit taller.

Some parents were so poor they sold their sons to chimney sweeps. The sweeps made the boys climb inside the chimneys of large houses and were known to light fires underneath slow or reluctant climbers. The practice of using boys to sweep chimneys was made illegal in 1832, but it continued until Lord Shaftesbury brought it to the attention of the government in the 1870s.

Oh no! Not smoky bacon again.

In 1870 the Education Act resulted in board-schools being set up across the country. Parents had to pay a penny every Monday to send their children to these schools but, in 1891, the charge was dropped and education was made compulsory.

Shaftesbury's Interesting Bits

Lord Shaftesbury (1801-1885) was born into a wealthy family but he worked hard to improve conditions for poor people. He was bullied at school and cried when he had to go, but cried again when he had to return home because his parents neglected him. Perhaps this is why he spent so much time working for children. He is accepted as one of the great reformers, but it wasn't easy and it took over thirty years to get a law to protect child sweeps.

Lord Shaftesbury

The Ragged Schools were set up to educate poor children and some Shaftesbury homes are still in existence.

His first job as an M.P. was to investigate the lunacy laws. In those days, lunatics were chained to the walls and on Sundays, when the warders had a day off, they were just left, still chained up, until Monday.

Now, I'll be back on Monday. Don't run away.

Shaftesbury was disgusted by this and personally took food to the lunatics on Sundays whilst helping bring about reforms

The statue in Piccadilly Circus, unveiled as a memorial to Lord Shaftesbury in 1886, was supposed to be the Angel of Charity but became known as Eros, the Greek God of Love. It was designed by Alfred Gilbert but the builders didn't follow his instructions properly and the fountain overflowed. The critics hated it and poor Gilbert, heavily in debt, went to Belgium.

Interesting Bits about Rich Children

Rich children were expected to be "seen and not heard" and were often brought up by a nanny in a special nursery. Sometimes they were neglected by their parents who might only see them once a day.

Parents were keen to educate their children and so a lot of toys were educational. Girls embroidered and played with dolls' houses to learn about running a home and boys were given soldiers and guns so that they could learn about being soldiers - many wealthy young men paid to be officers in the army.

Both boys and girls played with clockwork toys, hoops and spinning tops. Toy theatres and clock-work trains were also very popular with boys.

A rocking horse was found in most nurseries.

Boys were either sent to school or taught at home by a tutor, but girls were nearly always taught at home by a governess. Boys were taught Latin, Greek and other subjects, but as every girl's ambition was to get married, they weren't taught very much.

Reading was enjoyed by all children and some children's books from Victorian times which are still on bookshelves today include "Black Beauty", "Treasure Island", "The Water Babies " and "Tom Brown's Schooldays".

He threw me!

25

Interesting War Bits

The Crimea is an area of Russia which projects into the Black Sea. It was the scene of battles between the Allies (Turkey, Britain and France) and Russia. The war, an example of appalling management and disorganisation, began when Russia invaded Turkey in 1854. Britain and France joined in to prevent Russia forcing her way into the Mediterranean.

Russia

Crimea

Romania

Bulgaria

Turkey

William Howard Russell from "The Times", was the first journalist to report from the scene of a war. He wrote that soldiers were fighting in snowy conditions without warm clothes, suffering because there were too few doctors, and dying because essential medical supplies were stranded just a few miles away. His readers were horrified and blamed the government which then asked Florence Nightingale to go and sort out the medical problems.

Two pieces of clothing appeared with the Crimean War. Lord Cardigan gave his name to the cardigan, and the balaclava helmet took its name from the port of Balaclava.

"How dare you? ! My lovely new cardigan!"

26

The Charge of the Light Brigade was a Crimean disaster when Lord Cardigan and 673 horse infantry attacked the wrong Russian guns. Under fire from three sides, they rode down the "Valley of Death" to put the guns out of action. 247 men were killed or wounded and Lord Tennyson later wrote a very famous poem about it under the imaginative title, "The Charge of the Light Brigade". Other battles were fought at Inkerman, Sebastopol and Balaclava. The Treaty of Paris finally ended the war in 1856.

The bravery of the common soldier became legendary and Victoria insisted on awarding some of the medals personally. This meant so much to the soldiers that many refused to hand in their medals for engraving as it was unlikely they would get the same one back. The only other positive result of the Crimean War was the work of Florence Nightingale.

I was brave in battle today.

In 1884, European countries shared out Africa. Britain took 16 countries including Ghana (then called the Gold Coast), Nigeria, Kenya (British East Africa) and Malawi (Nyasaland). Britain also shared Egypt; so that her foreign lands were then so extensive that people said the sun never set on her Empire.

The Egyptians resented being under foreign control but their rebellion was suppressed at the Battle of Tel-el-Kebir (1882) and a small British army was left to keep order.

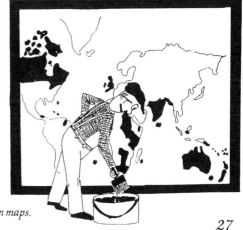

The British Empire was coloured pink on maps.

Observers in tethered air balloons were used to direct artillery during the Boer War.

Behind you!

In 1899 war broke out between Britain and the Transvaal, a state in South Africa, which was controlled by Dutch farmers known as Boers. Everyone thought that the farmers would easily be beaten, but it was 1902 before the Boers were finally defeated.

Britain had developed strong trade bases in India and controlled a large part of the country.

However, the British rulers treated the Indians insensitively and in 1857 Indian soldiers mutinied after being given gun cartridges covered in grease made from the fat of pigs and cows; animals regarded as either unclean or sacred by Indian religions. The mutiny was quelled and in 1876 Victoria was proclaimed Empress of India. Sadly, the damage had been done and the British and Indians never got on as well again.

Victoria never went to India but she liked to pretend she was there.

To the south, Britain had forces in the Sudan and, when the Sudanese rebelled against their Egyptian rulers, the British government sent General Gordon to evacuate the British troops. Gordon decided not to retreat, but to fight the rebels and he asked for more men and arms. By the time the government had decided what to do, it was too late. The relief force arrived two days after Gordon had been beheaded by the rebels. In 1898, General Kitchener recaptured the Sudan.

Interesting Sporty Bits

Towards the end of the century, Victorians took more interest in outdoor activities as they rightly thought that it was good for their health. Naturally, it was the richer classes who had most time to enjoy themselves; the poor were too busy working.

New sports included squash, invented by the pupils of Harrow School in 1850, basketball invented in America in 1891, and in 1874, a game invented by Major Walter C. Wingfield. He called it "Sphairistike" which is Greek for 'ball-game', but thankfully the name

was later changed to lawn-tennis. The first Wimbledon championship (gentlemen's singles only) was held in 1877 at the club which originally catered for the gentler game of croquet.

Fanthy a thet of thrairithtike?

Ladies had to wear long dresses for tennis and gentlemen wore top hats to play cricket, but, as the popularity of active sports grew, clothing became more appropriate. Ladies rode horse-back side-saddle until about 1880 and when cycling clubs sprang up this produced another example of a sport where ladies' clothing had to change. Other popular sports for ladies were archery and croquet (where their crinolines made for easy cheating).

Don't know how she always gets ahead.

Football was played in the streets and was extremely rough until the first definite rules appeared with the creation of the Football Association in 1863. Fifteen teams played for the first F.A. Cup in 1871.

In 1896, after a break of 1500 years, the Olympic Games were reinstated in Athens. It was the idea of one man and, surprisingly, he had quite a task persuading others that it was a good idea. The 1896 games were rather different to the modern games as only men competed. There were just twelve events, one of which was rope-climbing.

Rekindling the Olympic flame.

Horse-riding had always been popular and Victoria was a very keen and able horse-woman, preferring to ride difficult horses because it gave her something to do. She often had her portrait painted on horse-back because it made her seem taller than she really was.

Horse-racing provided a day out where all the classes brushed shoulders. The Epsom Derby attracted particularly large crowds.

Swimming was a well-liked pastime, particularly as so many people went to the sea-side for day-trips and holidays, but swimming was very different then. Bathing machines, in which swimmers could change and reach the water without being seen, were a common sight.

It was also quite normal to be dunked a few times under the water by a woman known as a 'dipper'. Once in the water, men and women weren't allowed to swim together, and anyone who tried to row over for a look was also stopped.

A Big Dipper

30

W.G. Grace was the most well-known Victorian cricketer. He was once bowled out for a duck but refused to leave the pitch, saying that the people had come to see him play, and see him play they would! During his long career, he scored an incredible 54,896 runs. Another famous cricketing moment was when England lost the Test to Australia for the first time. The stumps were burnt and an announcement was placed in The Times saying that English cricket had died and the ashes would be taken to Australia. The two countries have been playing for the Ashes ever since.

The upper classes travelled to Henley-on-Thames to see the rowing in the new Henley Royal Regatta, which was founded in 1839 to attract more visitors to the little town.

In 1862, the British in India enjoyed playing Polo, a game from the Punjab. Its name comes from the Tibetan word "pulu" which means willowroot. Another game which developed in India was snooker.

Waiting for Matthew Webb.

In 1875, Matthew Webb was the first man to swim the English Channel. It took him 21 hours and 45 minutes to swim the 38 miles, a long time when you consider that the fastest swimmer so far is a woman who took less than 8 hours!

31

Interesting Christmas Bits

Many of the traditions we enjoy today were begun by the Victorians; they loved Christmas and made it into a real family celebration. Albert popularised the Christmas tree, which would have been decorated with real candles.

"I'll kill him"!

When Christmas cards first appeared in the 1840s, they were too expensive for most people. However, the habit of sending cards grew and affordable printed cards were being sold in the shops by the 1870s, all helped along by the special halfpenny Christmas stamp issued by the Post Office in 1870.

Dickens' story "A Christmas Carol" describes a snowy, white Christmas. This wasn't just his vivid imagination as there were a number of very cold and snowy Christmasses when he was alive. His novel promotes the idea of generosity and kindness at Christmas and many Victorians shared this.

Presents were generally opened on Christmas Eve, and Boxing Day (the first working day after Christmas day) was the day that rich people gave Christmas boxes to their servants and tradesmen.

The practice of hanging stockings at the end of the bed originated from a foreign legend, but in Britain it was the Victorians who made it popular.

Queen Victoria rewarded her cook by dropping sovereigns into the uncooked Christmas pudding mixture.

A large number of popular songs and carols were composed in Victorian times including "Jingle Bells", "Once in Royal David's City", "We Three Kings of Orient Are" and "Hark the Herald Angels Sing" which was composed by Mendelssohn.

Fa la la la la

In 1844, a sweet-shop owner called Tom Smith sold sugared almonds in twists of tissue paper. They sold so well that he decided to put love messages in with them. Then, inspired by a crackling fire, he experimented with chemicals and cardboard and made the first real Christmas cracker.

I think we might have overdone it!

Pantomime was a tradition that was nearly killed by Victorian music hall. However, it managed to survive and the pantomime dame is a direct result of the music hall influence.

Law and Order Bits

The most infamous Victorian criminal was Jack the Ripper who murdered five prostitutes in the London's East End in 1888. The murders were particularly gruesome because the victims were also cut up and bits of them sent to the police.

The Ripper was never caught, although there were rumours that a clairvoyant identified him as an aristocratic doctor. The police generally discounted anyone "respectable" so aristocratic murderers had more chance of getting away with their crimes.

The one on the left has a top hat, so it must be the one on the right.

The first police, known as Peelers, were created by the Home Secretary, Robert Peel, in 1829, and in 1842 a small detective force was set up. However, working undercover was seen as underhand and not proper behaviour for Englishmen.

In 1833, a police sergeant, William Popay, was the focus of a public outcry after he disguised himself as an artist to investigate a crime. He was dismissed from the police service and it was many years before undercover work was accepted.

We're not that sort of Special Branch!

Policemen could be sacked for going undercover.

Victorian methods of detection were very basic, with inefficient records (most criminals just changed their names once released from prison) and no finger-printing. Scotland Yard only got its first telephone in 1901. Photography was used not only to identify criminals but also, in one Ripper case, the victim's eyes were photo-graphed as people believed that the last thing she had seen would be imprinted on them

She was hit by the number nine bus.

Criminals as young as five years old were sent to prison and in the 1840s more than 55 new prisons were built. The old Newgate prison attracted huge crowds to public hangings until 1868 after which executions were held inside the prison. Conditions inside were appalling and Elizabeth Fry, the great prison reformer, frequently visited Newgate, where she found 300 women in just four rooms. Some of them had even had to sell their clothes for food.

Newgate prison was the scene of hangings until 1901.

Now ladies, who will give me 2 pairs of knickers for this lovely fruit?

Convicts were expected to work, even if the work was pointless. For example, inmates of the Clerkenwell House of Correction picked pieces of rope apart or spent hours on a treadmill connected to absolutely nothing.

Interesting Writers' Bits

Reading was a good way to pass the time, and a number of great writers were Victorians, amongst them George Eliot (who was a woman writing under a male pen-name), Anthony Trollope (who invented the post-box), the Brontë sisters, Wilkie Collins, Mrs. Gaskell and Rudyard Kipling who wrote "The Jungle Book" in 1894.

Charles Dickens

Charles Dickens (1812-1870) was one of the most important Victorian writers. Most of his novels were published in magazines and it could take 18 months for readers to get to the last instalment. Dickens was angry that the poor were treated so cruelly and, through his books, brought their plight to the public's attention.

He was a workaholic, probably because his father was twice sent to prison for debt and Charles was determined that this should not happen to him.

His most famous works include "Oliver Twist" and "A Christmas Carol" which features the miserly Scrooge.

Bob Cratchit's character was based on personal experience; at the age of 16, Dickens worked from 7 a.m. to 9 p.m. in a lawyer's office.

Robert Louis Stevenson (1850-1894) wrote "Kidnapped", "Dr. Jekyll and Mr. Hyde" and "Treasure Island". He was born in Edinburgh and trained to be a lawyer although he always wanted to write. His family disowned him because they disapproved of his friends and disliked his bad manners.

Sherlock Holmes was a fictional character in detective stories written by Sir Arthur Conan Doyle (1859-1930). Conan Doyle was a failed doctor who turned to writing to support himself and his family. He later became an enthusiastic spiritualist, communicating with dead relatives and declaring his total belief in the existence of fairies.

Thomas Hardy (1840-1928) trained as an architect before writing novels and poetry about rural Dorset. He also wrote about sexual relationships, which many Victorians found unacceptable and his editors often requested changes before agreeing to publish. Even so, his last novel, "Jude the Obscure", was nick-named "Jude the Obscene" and publicly burnt by a Bishop.

I hate wearing this stupid dress!

"Alice's Adventures in Wonderland" was written by Lewis Carroll (1832-1898). In fact he was the Reverend Charles Dodgson but he was an Oxford academic who rarely preached. Lots of his friends were children and he wrote the story for a little girl called Alice. Dodgson was also well-known as the greatest Victorian child-photographer.

Victoria was very taken by the "Alice" stories and ordered all of Dodgson's other works. She was very disappointed to find they were all about maths and astronomy in which he was a lecturer.

Interesting Building Bits

Poo!

Lord Nelson's victory at the Battle of Trafalgar (1805) was finally commemorated in 1830 when Trafalgar Square was given its name. Nelson's 16-ton statue was hoisted onto its column in 1843, but it wasn't cleaned until 1905 when four tons of pigeon droppings were removed.

Sir Edwin Landseer modelled the lions at the base of the column. He painted Victoria's portrait many times and was a very famous artist, but Parliament decided not to buy his famous painting "The Monarch of the Glen".

As London grew, more river crossings were needed and the most famous of the Victorian bridges, Tower Bridge, opened in 1894. It was designed to harmonise with the adjacent Tower of London, hence the towers and turrets. Soon after it was built, the bridge was being opened up to 40 times a day to allow ships to pass into the Port of London. This has now dropped to just a few times a week. The bridge was raised by massive steam engines which were operated by a team of 80 men. In 1976, after almost 90 years of steam, electric motors took over.

Tower Bridge

Have you been yet?

Prince Albert's Great Exhibition (1851) was housed in the biggest glass structure ever seen. It was called the Crystal Palace and was built in Hyde Park where it stayed for the six-month exhibition. As the building was erected over existing trees, many of the exhibits were "decorated" by the local birds. After the exhibition, the Crystal Palace was moved to Sydenham where it burnt down in 1936.

The Houses of Parliament and the tower of Big Ben were built in 1840-1850 because earlier buildings had been destroyed by fire in 1834. Not far away in South Kensington, the Royal Albert hall was built as a memorial to the Prince Consort. Albert had planned a collection of museums in the area which was sometimes referred to as Albertopolis. The Victoria and Albert, Science and Natural History museums are just some of the many educational institutions in the area.

Big Ben

The Royal Albert Hall

Queen Victoria took a great personal interest in the building of the Albert Hall. She said it was like the British constitution because "it is large, all-embracing and extremely confusing to those who are not familiar with it."

Interesting Inventions and Discoveries

Victoria's reign was the age of machines and hundreds of new inventions, some more useful than others, were introduced during her 60 years on the throne. Useful inventions included the first toilet cistern, invented by Thomas Crapper in 1900, the wireless (Marconi, 1901) and the telephone (Alexander Graham Bell, 1876).

Come quick, it's "The Archers".

The first postage stamps, thought up by a schoolteacher named Rowland Hill, were used in 1840. The idea proved so popular that the post office decided they needed collection boxes in the streets. The designer of one early box forgot to leave a space for the letter slot, so rather than spoil the pattern, someone had the bright idea of putting the slot in the top. Unfortunately, a slot in the top let the rain in and made everything soggy.

The sewing machine had been invented once before but had been smashed by angry workers who feared for their jobs. It arrived again, this time to stay, in the 1840s. Another invention to affect clothing was the zip (1891, Judson Whitcomb).

In its early days the zip was rather unreliable.

Thomas Alva Edison was an American who was responsible for thousands of inventions including the light bulb (1879) and the phonograph (1877) which eventually evolved into the record player.

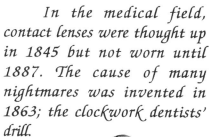

In the medical field, contact lenses were thought up in 1845 but not worn until 1887. The cause of many nightmares was invented in 1863; the clockwork dentists' drill.

A Mr. Macintosh worked out a way to get a rubbery, waterproof substance between layers of cloth. He made the cloth into a raincoat and the Macintosh was born in 1823.

Refrigeration was the subject of considerable research but fridges for the home didn't appear until after 1910. To keep food fresh, Victorians cut ice from frozen lakes and packed it in straw. This would last the whole summer.

In 1901, H.C. Booth invented the vacuum cleaner. The machine, which had to be pulled by a horse, remained outside the home being cleaned and the hose was fed through the windows.

Michael Faraday (1791-1867) specialised in working with electricity. He invented the electric motor and the transformer.

Finally, a selection of Victorian inventions includes barbed wire (Glidden, 1873), plastic (Parkes, 1862), escalators (Reno, 1894), steam-powered airships (Giffard, 1852), submarines (1863) and dynamite (Nobel, 1840).

Interesting Leisure Bits

Victorians found plenty of ways to pass their time and enjoyed dancing, painting, playing cards and billiards, reading, gambling, visiting the zoo and going to the waxworks.

Upper class families might visit the opera, but not the theatre as this had become rather rough and was considered suitable only for the lower classes. Victorian families (which on average had 5.8 children) could also watch a hanging, or visit a freak show at a travelling fair.

Victorian families were big - on average 5.8 children in each.

Freaks included oddities like the "Living Skeleton" and the "Pig-Faced Lady" who was really a dressed bear with a shaved face. The animal was tied to a chair in gloomy light and visitors would pay to see the "lady". The bear was eventually rescued, but rat-pits, badger-baiting and cock-fighting remained popular long after they were made illegal in the middle of the century.

The pig-faced lady was really a dressed-up bear.

The average Victorian didn't have much free time but in 1847 the Factory Act gave workers Saturday afternoons off and in 1871 four Bank Holidays a year were introduced.

Optical toys were popular with the whole family and kaleidoscopes and magic lantern shows were all the rage. Photography and moving pictures were also developing quickly and by the end of the century, short films were attracting crowds.

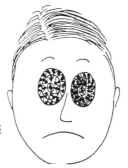

The effects of looking through a kaleidoscope for too long.

Queen Victoria watched a ten-minute film of her diamond jubilee procession and said that, apart from tiring her eyes and giving her a headache, it was a marvel!

Until 1859 it was compulsory to celebrate Guy Fawkes Night and, even when it became optional, watching fireworks remained a popular activity.

Oooh! Aaah!

Tourism began when railways made long-distance travel possible. Thomas Cook started his travel company by taking a group of workers to a temperance meeting (all about the evils of drink). In 1851, he took his first group abroad to Paris, but most people stayed in Britain and went to the sea-side. Resorts boomed; piers and promenades were built, and donkey rides and Punch and Judy shows were common.

Interesting Clothes Bits

Victoria's long reign saw many different styles, but the crinoline was a popular and long-lived fashion. Ladies wore multiple petticoats to make their skirts fuller and eventually steel frames were used to hold the material out even further. Most ladies were delighted to wear a frame as it meant fewer hot and heavy underclothes, but Florence Nightingale refused to use one, preferring her old horsehair petticoats. Surprisingly, under such austere outerwear, highly patterned socks were common; Victoria had her initials embroidered on hers.

Big knickers and jazzy socks were part of Victorian life.

A small waist was essential for the fashion-conscious, so ladies squeezed themselves into corsets. Some even had their lower ribs removed to achieve a thinner waist!

Wide skirts weren't very practical however, especially for riding bicycles and horses, so Amelia Bloomer's divided skirt (or "Bloomers") should have been well-received. It wasn't, and skirts, whether wide or narrow, remained the accepted costume for many years.

Him; "Where's your bike?"
Her; "I'm riding it".

A tanned skin was thought to be a sign that you were working-class because only outdoor workers got tanned. To keep the sun off their complexions, ladies carried parasols, which may be the reason why sunglasses didn't catch on when they were introduced in 1885.

Men wore formal suits and hats for most of Victoria's reign, although tight-fitting breech type trousers became looser and more patterned, and the cravat gave way to a narrower tie.

Na na ni na na, we can see your knickers.

Little girls' clothes resembled ladies' clothes, except that they wore no knickers, just long drawers which were designed to show beneath their dresses. Boys' clothes were nothing like their fathers' and, until the age of 5, boys wore dresses and had long hair. In many old photos, it's difficult to tell boys from girls.

After the age of 5, boys were allowed to wear breeches and for a while the sailor-suit was very fashionable.

Swimming costumes were designed to cover the whole body and were made of a wool mix which was extremely heavy once wet. Until ladies started bathing men swam in the nude.

In America in 1874, Levi Strauss made some work-trousers from left-over tent material and invented jeans. It's likely that jeans were so-called because the cotton came from Genoa but also possible that denim was named after the French town of Nimes.

Famous People's Interesting Bits

Charles Darwin (1809-1882) travelled widely, studying nature. He sailed all over the world in "Beagle" and discovered lots of new species of animals and plants. He also wrote a book, "On the Origin of Species", in which he said that humans were descended from apes, not God. Religious Victorians were furious because they thought Darwin was saying that the Bible was wrong.

Can't see his reasoning myself.

Samuel Plimsoll M.P. (1824-98) found out that owners were overloading their ships, knowing that they could claim insurance money if the ships sank. The sailors called them "coffin ships". Plimsoll tried, in vain, to get M.P.s to discuss this before finally losing his temper and shouting "You're a lot of damned murderers" at them. This stirred them into action and the ensuing law required a "Plimsoll line" to be drawn around every ship; if the ship was overloaded, the line disappeared under water.

Gym shoes were called plimsolls because of the line between the upper and the sole.

William Gladstone (1809-1898) was a Liberal prime minister. He wanted peace and freedom for all countries and tried, unsuccessfully, to give Ireland their own government. Gladstone was a very thorough man. He once spoke for 8 hours in parliament and he sent Queen Victoria 12 pages of detailed notes as a summary of a bill. She was bored and confused by his long explanations and thoroughly disliked him.

Benjamin Disraeli (1804-81) was one of Victoria's favourite prime ministers. He flattered her by calling her his "Fairy Queen" and he suggested the title," Empress of India". He was an unusual Conservative, coming from a Jewish family and having attended neither public school nor university. He also liked to wear rings and highly coloured, embroidered clothes.

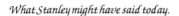

What Stanley might have said today.

"Yo! Dave! How ya' doin'?"

David Livingstone (1813-1873) crossed Africa as a missionary and explorer. He preached Christianity, fought slavery and disapproved of alcohol (unless he was drinking it). He appeared to care little for his family which he left often and for long periods. Livingstone discovered Lake Nyasa (now Lake Malawi) and Victoria Falls before he disappeared in 1865. By then, he was so famous that an American newspaper sent Mr. Stanley, another explorer, to find him. They met in Ujiji (present-day Tanzania) where Stanley uttered the famous words, "Dr. Livingstone, I presume". Livingstone died in Africa and his two servants carried his body one thousand miles to Zanzibar.

William Morris (1834-1896) made a huge impact on the art world. He was a skilled stone-carver and carpenter as well as a painter and he wanted to resurrect the old crafts. Morris based his patterns on nature and his designs appeared on everything from wallpaper to pottery. They are still widely used today.

47

Interesting Bits of Food

A typical Victorian take-away would have been baked potatoes, pies and roast chestnuts, all cooked on the street. In summer, ice-cream was very popular and the muffin man was a welcome sight at any time of the year. Definitely not a take-away food however, was jelly which was a firm Victorian favourite.

There's something very odd about this bread.

Some foods had unexpected ingredients as there were no laws to prevent food being spoiled. To make bigger profits, tradesmen were known to add water to milk and plaster of Paris to flour.

Although 'eating chocolate' was invented in 1828, the first chocolate bars weren't seen in Britain until the 1840s. Mr. Cadbury is famous for his chocolate and also for caring about his workforce. He built a model village for them, called Bournville, and provided them with decent working conditions.

In 1869, to combat the effects of a butter shortage, somebody thought of mixing chopped cow's udder, skimmed milk and solid beef fat so making margarine.

Canned food, which had been around since 1811, was being used by the services in the 1860s, but the cans were sealed with lead solder, a very poisonous substance which contaminated the food and poisoned the consumer. Another problem with canned food was that no one invented the can-opener until 1855. Until then, cans had to be opened with a hammer and chisel.

Couldn't we just have fruit?

Family Tree

George III   =   Charlotte of
r.1760-1820   Mecklenburg-Strelitz d.1818

William IV   Edward, Duke of Kent d.1820
r.1830-1837   m.Victoria of Saxe-Coburg

Victoria   =   Albert
r.1837-1901

| Victoria (Vicky) 1840-1901 | Edward VII (Bertie) 1841-1910 | Alice 1843-78 | Alfred (Affie) 1844-1900 | Helena 1846-1923 | Louise 1848-1939 | Arthur 1850-1942 | Leopold 1853-84 | Beatrice (Baby) 1857-1944 |

Index